WHAT SHOULD
I WEAR
TO WORK?

Jana Sedláčková
Alexandra Májová

Albatros

chef's hat

bandana

white gloves

black jacket with two rows of buttons

white jacket with two rows of buttons

black-and-white checked trousers

oven mitts

wooden spoon

slip-on shoes

neatly folded napkin

book of family recipes

large pot

ladle

chef's apron

tea towel

sharp knife

rolling pin

tasting spoon

bowl of ingredients

pasta tongs

chopping board

frying pan

work trousers with bib

work trousers without bib

apron

short-sleeved T-shirt

shorts with pockets

rake

spade

farm boots

short gloves for light work

long gloves for hard work

hardwearing socks

flannel shirt

rain boots

headscarf

sunhat

kneepads

hoe

straw hat

flowerpot

bag of seeds

trowel

watering can

pruning clippers

metronome

white shirt

white bow-tie

decorative pin with pearl

tailcoat

vest

little black lace dress

blouse with tie

black stockings

jacket with decorative embroidery

high-waisted pants with white suspenders

music stand

patent-leather shoes with bows

tuning fork

baton

black polo turtleneck

velvet sweater

blouse with tie

down winter coat

crampons (shoe spikes for ice climbing)

thermos flask

thermal underwear

overgloves and undergloves (waterproof)

neck warmer

wool sweater

thermal pants

fur hat with earflaps

protective mask

wool socks

winter boots for extreme conditions

whistle

dried food, energy bars

GPS tracker

ice axe

snowshoes

snow shovel

skis

firefighter's helmet

Protective coat with many smart sensors

firefighter's uniform

sturdy boots

nonflammable gloves

nonflammable pants

rescue belt with snap hook

breathing apparatus

flashlight

heavy, fire-resistant suit

nonflammable underwear

chemical-resistant suit

firefighter's hose

walkie-talkie

crowbar

fire extinguisher

firefighter's axe

firefighter's ladder

leotard with waistband

leotard with skirt

leotard with lace

lightweight ballet dress

long tulle skirt

pointe shoes

ballet slippers

stirrup legwarmers

embroidered ballet dress with sleeves

hair clips

tiara

ballet tights

headband with feathers

hairnet

ribbon choker

makeup

long gloves

jumpsuit

high-visibility jumpsuit

baseball cap

rubber boots

rubber gloves

overalls

polo shirt

squeegee

sponge

bucket of soapy water

vacuum car-cleaner

waterproof work boots

washing mitt

wheel-cleaning brush

high-pressure washer

small towel

window cleaner

ice scraper

bodywork polisher

pencil skirt and short-sleeved blouse

elegant skirt

pleated skirt

pantsuit

formal trousers

tweed dress with collar

watch

notepad

long-sleeved blouse

nylons

handbag

telephone

dress shoes

desk calendar

laptop

button-up cardigan

paper clips

high-heels

flat shoes with bows

stapler

sheets of paper

binders

top with necklace

white coat with pockets

medical shirt

fun tunic with kittens

medical dress

work skirt

fleece vest

stethoscope

orthopedic shoes

scalpel

surgical mask

hypodermic syringe

medical pants

rubber gloves

thermometer

scrubs

medic's hat

medication

transfusion apparatus

scissors

antibacterial footwear

ECG (electrocardiogram) machine

hat

elegant neckerchief

travel coat with scarf

vest

white gloves

blouse

tight-fitting dress

sunglasses

flight tickets

headset with microphone

jacket

knee-length pencil skirt

high-visibility vest

airplane earrings

earplugs

snack tray

high-heels

life vest

suitcase

oxygen mask

overalls

white cap

heat-resistant gloves

chimney sweep's suit

black cap

safety helmet

short black jacket

top hat

white neckerchief

black shoes

brushes (long and short)

chimney-cleaning brush with reel

soot box

chimney inspection mirror

flashlight

wire brush

shovel

cleaning stick with chimney brush

hemp rope

smoke tester

fire-extinguishing tool

roof ladder

WHAT SHOULD
I WEAR
TO WORK?

Jana Sedláčková
Alexandra Májová

© B4U Publishing for Albatros,
an imprint of Albatros Media Group, 2023
5. května 1746/22, Prague 4, Czech Republic
Written by Jana Sedláčková
Illustrations © Alexandra Májová
Translated by Andrew Oakland
Edited by Scott Alexander Jones

Printed in China by Leo Paper Group